# Best-Loved Piano Classics

## 36 Favorite Works
## by 22 Great Composers

Selected and Edited by
Ronald Herder

DOVER PUBLICATIONS, INC.
Mineola, New York

*Bibliographical Note*

This Dover edition, first published in 2001, is a new compilation of works originally published separately in early authoritative editions.

*International Standard Book Number: 0-486-41378-0*

Manufactured in the United States of America
Dover Publications, Inc., 31 East 2nd Street, Mineola, N.Y. 11501

# CONTENTS

# ALPHABETICAL LIST OF TITLES

# Best-Loved
# Piano Classics

# Leyenda (Asturias)
*Legend from Asturias*

Prelude from *Songs of Spain*, Op. 232 (1896)

Isaac Albéniz
(Spain, 1860–1909)

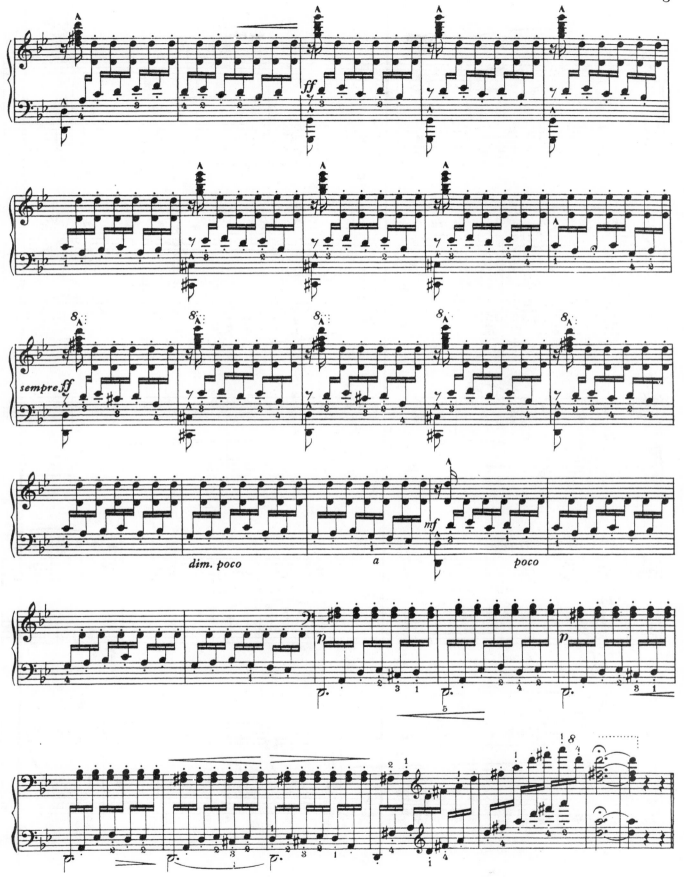

**Tempo I.**

*marcato il canto*

# Chromatic Fantasia and Fugue

BWV 903 (*ca.* 1720, revised *ca.* 1730)

Johann Sebastian Bach
(Germany, 1685–1750)

**Fantasia.**

Fuga.

# Prelude in F minor

*Well-Tempered Clavier,* Book II, No. 12 / BWV 881 (1744)

Johann Sebastian Bach

# "Jesu, Joy of Man's Desiring"

Chorale from Cantata 147 (1717)

*Keyboard reduction from the full score by Ronald Herder*

Johann Sebastian Bach

# "Pathétique" Sonata

Second movement of Sonata No. 8 in C minor, Op. 13 (1798–9)

Ludwig van Beethoven
(Germany & Austria, 1770–1827)

**Adagio cantabile.**

# "Rage Over a Lost Penny"

Rondo a capriccio, Op. 129 (1795)

Ludwig van Beethoven

34

# "Edward" Ballade

No. 1 of *Four Ballades,* Op. 10 (1854) / From the Scottish ballad "Edward"

Johannes Brahms
(Germany & Austria, 1833–1897)

38

# Hungarian Dance No. 3
## in F major

From *21 Hungarian Dances* for piano four hands (1852–69)

Johannes Brahms

*Solo piano arrangement by the composer (1872)*

# Intermezzo in A major

No. 2 of six *Piano Pieces*, Op. 118 (1892)

Johannes Brahms

# Etude in E major

No. 3 of twelve *Etudes*, Op. 10 (1832)

Frédéric Chopin
(Poland & France, 1810–1849)

# "Revolutionary" Etude

Etude in C minor, No. 12 of twelve *Etudes,* Op. 10 (1830)

Allegro con fuoco.

Frédéric Chopin

# Nocturne in E minor

Op. 72, No. 1 (1827)

Frédéric Chopin

# Fantasie-Impromptu
## in C-sharp minor
### Op. 66 (1835)

Frédéric Chopin

Allegro agitato.

Tempo I.(Allegro agitato.)

65

# The Sunken Cathedral

*La Cathédrale engloutie,* No. 10 of twelve *Preludes,* Book I (1909–10)

Claude Debussy
(France, 1862–1918)

*)The direction ♩=♩ should appear over the barline between mm. 6 and 7; it should be canceled by the direction ♩=♩ over the barline between mm. 12 and 13. (This faster tempo in mm. 7–12, and later in mm. 22–83, can be heard on Debussy's piano-roll recording of this prelude.)

**Peu à peu sortant de la brume**

Un peu moins lent (Dans une expression allant grandissant)

*pp expressif et concentré*

au Mouvement

Dans la sonorité du début

*)The direction ♩=♩ should appear over the barline between mm. 83 and 84.

# The Maiden with the Flaxen Hair

*La fille aux cheveux de lin*, No. 8 of twelve *Preludes*, Book I (1909–10)

Claude Debussy

# Slavonic Dance in E minor

No. 2 of eight *Slavonic Dances*, Op. 46 (1878)

*Originally scored for piano four hands*

Antonín Dvořák
(Czechoslovakia, 1841–1904)

# Morning Mood

From incidental music to Henrik Ibsen's play *Peer Gynt*, Op. 23 (1874–5)

*Transcribed by the composer from his orchestral suite*

Edvard Grieg
(Norway, 1843–1907)

85

# Åse's Death

From incidental music to Henrik Ibsen's play *Peer Gynt*, Op. 23 (1874–5)

Edvard Grieg

*Transcribed by the composer from his orchestral suite*

# Norwegian Dance No. 2

From four *Norwegian Dances* for piano four hands, Op. 35 (1881)

Edvard Grieg

*Transcribed by the composer for solo piano*

# Andante with Variations
## in F minor

"A Little Divertimento" (1793)

Joseph Haydn
(Austria, 1732–1809)

*Edited by Xaver Scharwenka*

FINALE

# "The Harmonious Blacksmith"
## Air and Five Variations

George Frideric Handel
(Germany & England, 1685–1759)

Posthumously bestowed nickname for a portion of the *Fifth Harpichord Suite* in E major (1720)

Air.

Var. 1.

Var. 2.

Var. 3.

Var. 4.

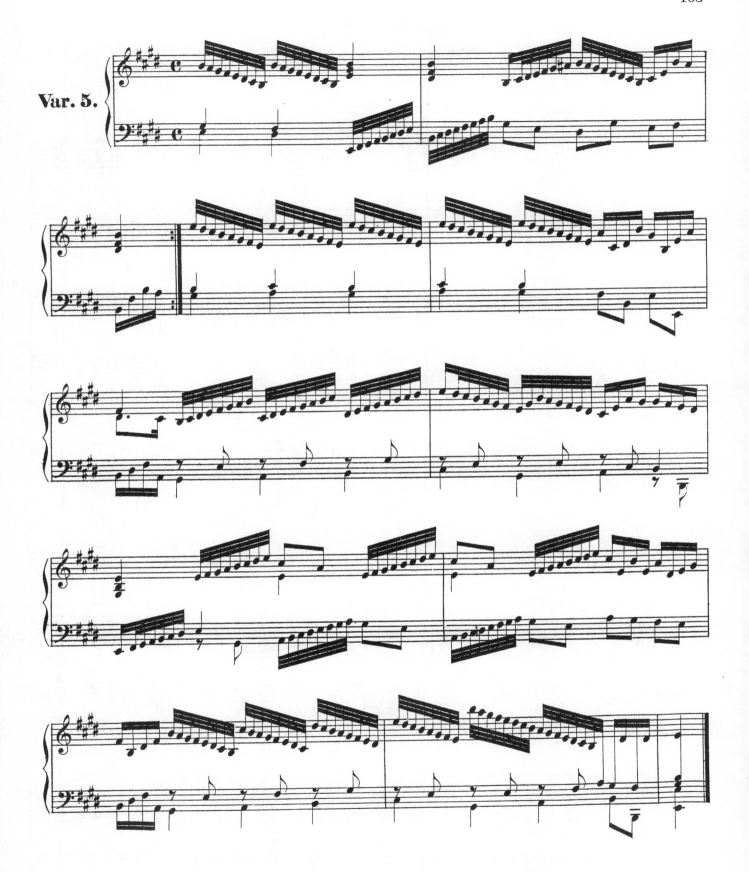

# Valse Oubliée No. 1

From *Three Forgotten Waltzes* (1881)

Franz Liszt
(Hungary & Germany, 1811–1886)

# Rondo capriccioso
## in E major

Op. 14 (1824)

Felix Mendelssohn
(Germany, 1809–1847)

# Scherzo in E minor

No. 2 of *Three Fantasias or Capriccios*, Op. 16 (1829)

Felix Mendelssohn

sempre Ped.

# Serenata

No. 1 of *Six Piano Pieces,* Op. 15 (1880?)

Moritz Moszkowski
(German of Polish descent, 1854–1925)

# Theme and 12 Variations
## on the French folk song "Ah! vous dirai-je, maman"

K265 (1781–2) / Later catalogued as K300e

Wolfgang Amadeus Mozart
(Austria, 1756–1791)

VAR. VI.

130

**VAR. XI.**
Adagio.

**VAR. XII.**
Allegro.

# Fantasy No. 3 in D minor

K397 (1782 or 1786–7) / Later catalogued as K385g

Wolfgang Amadeus Mozart

# Hopak of the Merry Young Ukranians

National dance from the comic opera *The Fair at Sorochintsy* (1874–80)

*Transcribed by the composer for solo piano*

Modest Mussorgsky
(Russia, 1839–1881)

# Melody in F

No. 1 of *Two Melodies,* Op. 3 (1852)

Anton Rubinstein
(Russia, 1829–1894)

# Sonata in E major

*Capriccio, K380*

Domenico Scarlatti
(Italy, 1685–1757)

# Polish National Dance No. 1
## in E-flat minor

From *16 Polish National Dances,* Op. 3 (1869)

Xaver Scharwenka
(Poland & Germany, 1850–1924)

# Impromptu in G-flat major

No. 3 of *Four Impromptus*, Op. 90 (1827?)

Franz Schubert
(Austria, 1797–1828)

# Arabesque

Op. 18 (1838)

Robert Schumann
(Germany, 1810–1856)

Leicht und zart
*Lightly and tenderly*

**Minore I**

**Etwas langsamer**
*Somewhat slower*

## Minore II

**Etwas langsamer.** *Somewhat slower, soft of touch, but strong in rhythm*

# Zum Schluss
### Ending

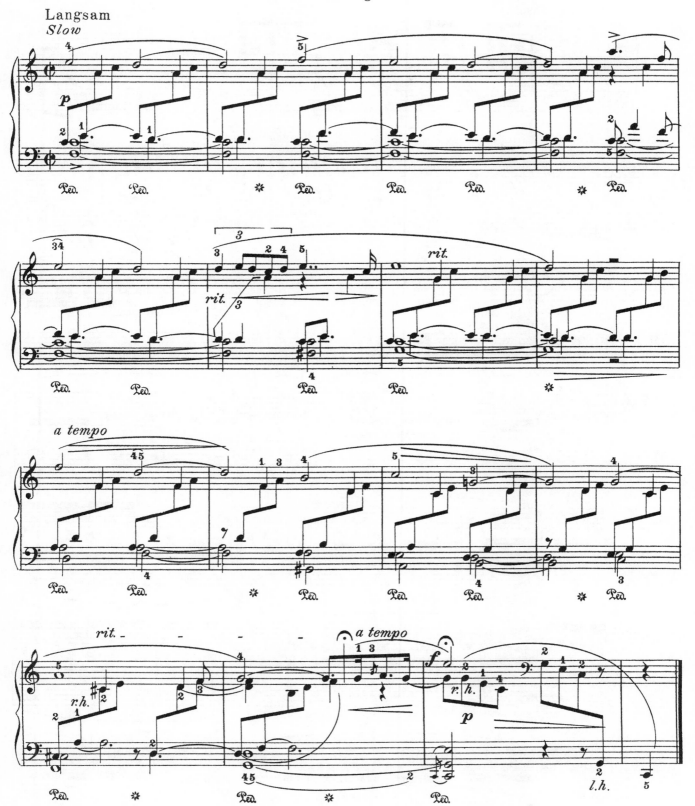

# Soaring

No. 2 of eight *Fantasy Pieces*, Op. 12 (1837)

Robert Schumann

# Tales from the Vienna Woods

Concert Waltz, Op. 325 (1868)

Johann Strauss
(Austria, 1825–1899)

**Introduction.**
Tempo di Valse.

(N. B. When for dancing leave out from A to B.)

# November: "In the Troïka"

No. 11 of *The Seasons*, Op. 37*bis*  (1875–6)

Peter Ilyitch Tchaikovsky
(Russia, 1840–1893)